The Spirit of the Female Warrior

This book is dedicate to my beautiful family, friends, and people I work with everyday~ reminding myself and others, that we all have the spirit of a warrior~

Compiled and Edited By Mary G. Madrigal, Ph.D.
Additional Editing- Richard H. Madrigal, Jr. and Corine Charm, LMFT
Cover Photo - magicalrecipesonline.com.

"The warrior spirit lies deep within us all.

It's a vital, rousing force that can turn the meek into the fearsome.

Women, as a tribe, are endowed with their own warrior instincts and powers, borne in the female psyche and biology."

~Melissa Soalt

-Pinterest.com

WE...

Never give up;

Never surrender;

Never Quit~

-Mary Madrigal

There Is A Positive Form of Being Selfish~

Be Selfish Enough to Take Care of Yourself First~

Then You Can Be of Service or Helpful to Others.

-Mary Madrigal

-Hdwallpapers360.com

Be truthful, Gentle and Fearless.

-Gandhi

-Taringa.net

Nothing is Stronger than You Are

~~Be Courageous

-Mary Madrigal

Sometimes the greatest battle we fight is within ourselves
-Author Unknown

-wall-pix.net

Embrace Your Strength and Know You Are Transforming Your Life~
-Mary Madrigal

Believe in Yourself And Focus on What Is Right with You and Your Life~
-Mary Madrigal

SOME TIMES...

You just have to pull up your

BIG GIRL PANTIES
And do it

Whether you want to or not.

-Pinterest.com

-Freelargeimages.com

I am a woman of strength
  Nothing can break my spirit
  I am a warrior of Light

    I am Me ~

-Unknown

You Were Put on This Earth to Achieve Your Greatest Self, to Live Out Your Purpose, and to do it Courageously.

-Dr. Steve Marabeli

-Wallpapersdb.org

-Fanpop.com

One Day the Battle Stopped and I Chose to See Myself the Way the Universe Created Me,

TO SHINE

-Pinterest.com

*Warriors are not born
And they are not made*

*Warriors create themselves
through trial and error,
pain and suffering,
and their ability to conquer
their own faults...*

-Pinterest.com

Be STRONG enough to stand alone,

SMART enough to Know When You Need Help,

And BRAVE enough to ask for it.

-Livehappylife.com

-Fanpop.com

-Elfessa.deviantart.com

I am friendly, kind, gentle, and loving but know that I have the strength to rise up and conquer all that life is tossing my way.

-Mary Madrigal

-Fanpop.com

Being Sensitive is a Great Quality.

It's So Much Better than Having a Cold Heart☺
-Mary Madrigal

Embrace Your Warrior Spirit

She is Always with You

Never Underestimate Your Strength

You Are a Beautiful Human Being

-Mary Madrigal

When Life Gives You Something That Makes You Feel AFRAID, That's When Life Gives You a Chance to BE BRAVE

-Lupytha Hermin

-Quoteko.com

-Flickr.com

Know that in every girl, there is a princess with strength of a warrior.

-Pinterest

The Stronger you become
The Gentler you Will Be
-Pinterest

-Fanpop.com

Everyone Needs a Self Care Day

What Can You Do Today To Nurture Yourself~

- Sleep in
- Manicure
- Pedicure
- Massage
- Nap
- Buy something pretty
- Take a Walk
- Play with your dog
- Have lunch with a friend
- Call a friend
- Go to the beach

-Photos-public-domain-com

How We Walk With the Broken or Wounded Speaks Louder Than

How We Sit With the Great
-Boldomatic.com

Today Reach Out To Someone You Love

-Hdscreen.me

Sometimes the strongest women Are the ones who love beyond all faults, cry behind closed doors, and fights battles that nobody knows about.

-BeautyforAshes

-Wallpaperup.com

You Have a Beautiful

Heart

Brave

And

Courageous

And Yet

So Gentle and Kind

Embrace Yourself

-Pinterest.com

I am a strong woman but every now and then, I also need someone to take my hand and say everything will be alright.

-The dailyquotes.com

-Pinterest.com

Some people think that to be strong is to never feel pain.

In reality, the strongest people are the ones who feel it, understand it, and accept it!

-Quotespictures.com

-nowwallpapers.blogspot.com

The brave woman is not the one who does not feel afraid, but she who conquers that fear.
-Nelson Mandela

-The warrior-goddess.blogspot.com

"Growth is painful, change is painful, but nothing is as painful as staying stuck somewhere you don't belong"

-Mandy Hale

"If you judge people, you have no time to love them."

-Mother Teresa

-Photoswithquotes.com

People who wonder whether the glass is half empty or half full miss the point.

The Glass is Refillable!
-Pinterest.com

-Pinterest.com

-fromtheirownlipswordpress.com

"Love yourself first And everything else falls in line. You really have to love yourself to get anything done in this world."
-Lucille Ball

Hold on and stay strong better things are coming
-quotehot.com

-Deligaris.deviantart

Warriors confront the conflict that most people refuse to acknowledge
-Bohdi Sanders

-Wallpaperhd.com

Together we stand side by side. There is nothing stronger than my spirit. I overcome challenges one by one.

-Mary Madrigal

The Rising Phoenix

You are Rising Up More Glorious Than Ever!

-Flywithmeproductions.com

Love, Mary

Please Visit My Website
www.phoenixrisinginstitute.org

www.ingramcontent.com/pod-product-compliance
Lightning Source LLC
Chambersburg PA
CBHW041744040426
42444CB00001B/20